whitestar kids

Amazing and True
Animal Heroes

Text by Leonardo Mazzeo
Illustrations by Bianca Austria

Contents

WELCOME!

Are you ready to begin an incredible journey?

You are about to read eighteen extraordinary stories; the protagonists are all animals, the most curious creatures in the world! These tales show them in the guise of heroes: from the cat who rescued her kittens to the orca who won his freedom, as well as such famous animals as Balto and Hachiko, whom you may have already heard of.

LET US SURPRISE YOU WITH THESE STORIES PUT INTO THEIR WORDS!

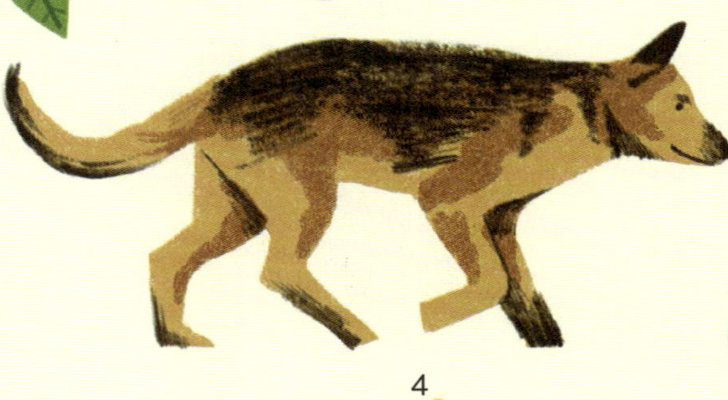

By the way, all the stories are absolutely true!

Although they may seem like fictional tales, the animals, with their unmistakable voices, will make you part of their beautiful and exciting stories, experienced by them firsthand. For example, a penguin will tell you how his wonderful relationship with a man in Brazil came about. He comes back to visit him every year, and the two remain friends! Can you imagine?
A penguin and a human are friends! And then there's a pigeon, a pig, a dolphin, and many other animals. You can count on it being an unforgettable trip!

Backpack on our shoulders, everything is ready . . . shall we start?

OFF WE GO ON OUR ADVENTURE...

Balto, the Unstoppable Sled Dog

The story of a the sled dog who became a symbol of teamwork, courage, tenacity, and hope.

I have to admit, I love the cold! I love it when the temperature drops below freezing and I can stay warm in my fur coat. I have it specifically to withstand the frigid temperatures of Alaska, the place where I live. One thing I like to do a lot is pull sleds; running to help my human friends is a major commitment.

I LOOK FORWARD TO MAKING MYSELF USEFUL!

That's why, when an epidemic broke out in a small, isolated town, I immediately came forward, barking and wagging my tail. I wanted to be the one pulling the sled!

It was a race against time. The inhabitants of that place lost in the ice were very sick, and neither planes nor trains could get there. It was January, and temperatures were reaching forty degrees below zero!

ONLY WE DOGS AND OUR DRIVERS COULD HOLD OUT.

Usually our job is to carry letters, but that time we were given a more important mission: to carry medicine to its destination. Our masters accepted the assignment, and we immediately followed them. We organized a relay race; the distance was long, more than 600 miles,

SO EVERYONE'S HELP WAS NEEDED!

And so my fellow sled dogs and I set to work, each taking over from time to time. When it was my turn, all that was left was the last stretch, more than fifty miles across the ice! They loaded my sled and I immediately started running. The icy air filled my lungs. I had my tongue hanging out from exhaustion. It was difficult, but I didn't give up.

I KNEW THAT SO MANY PEOPLE'S LIVES DEPENDED ON ME, AND I DIDN'T WANT TO LET MY HUMAN FRIENDS DOWN!

We managed to bring the medicine in time, and the epidemic was defeated. My name was in all the newspapers; praise for Balto was everywhere in the following days! They even dedicated a statue to me.

This pleases
me, but I want to say that
the credit for the feat is not mine
alone; many other sled dogs like me
helped carry the medicine!

THE ONE WHO RAN THE LONGEST DISTANCE
WAS MY FRIEND TOGO—WHAT A GOOD BOY!

He ran more than ninety miles, almost twice as far as
me. The real strength, however, came from the group;
no one would ever have been able to accomplish the
mission alone. All together, we were able to save
so many people.

HOORAY!

Dindim, the Grateful Penguin

The story of a penguin who returns each year to visit the man who saved his life.

One day many years ago I was swimming happily in the ocean, as I have always done. I like being in the water so much; it is full of friends to play with and fish to catch! I was having a great time then, too, until all of a sudden everything turned black. My vision had darkened, and my little wings were stuck to my body.

WHAT A DISASTER!

I could hardly move, and I could no longer see any of my companions. Where had everyone gone? What was happening to me? Suddenly I fainted. I don't know how much time passed; I only remember that I found myself on the beach. How had I ended up there?

I felt the warmth of
the sand beneath me
and breathed in the smell of the
ocean, but I couldn't see anything.
My eyes were sealed shut by a sticky black
substance, which had also
gotten into my mouth.

YUCK, HOW DISGUSTING!

I was very hungry and very tired. My strength
was deserting me. Then, suddenly, a pair of
gentle hands picked me up . . .

A good man took care of me;
he washed all the sticky oil off me,
fed me, and gave me a drink.

I WAS SO LUCKY
HE FOUND ME!

The man smiled at me every day and told me
incredible stories of places I had never been.
We became best friends.

After a few days I was back in full form, and my
new friend accompanied me to the beach.
I jumped in and finally felt the cool water enveloping
my penguin body—what a great feeling! I said
goodbye to the man who saved me,
but I did not forget about him. I return
to see him every year, together
with my companions.

HE IS NOW PART
OF OUR FAMILY.

Moko, the Unselfish Dolphin

The story of a dolphin who helped two other animals find their way home.

Being in the water is what I like most. I spend my days with my dolphin friends, and we have a lot of fun! Together we laugh, we swim great distances, we dive into the depths of the ocean and then quickly come back up to the surface and jump out of the water! When people see us, they laugh with us and shout,

"LOOK, THAT'S MOKO WITH HIS FRIENDS!"

Once, while swimming near the coast, I noticed something strange. There were two small whales on the beach. Instead of being in the ocean they were on the sand.

OH NO, HOW SCARY!

We cetaceans need oxygen to breathe, it's true, but our life is in the water, and when we are out of it we suffer a lot!

Some humans were trying to help the two little whales; at a certain point they even managed to get them back into the water; shortly after, however, the current pushed them back to shore.

At that point I said to myself, I must do something!
So I called out to them loudly:

"WHALES! WHALES! THIS WAY!"

They turned and looked at me with surprise; I had never seen two animals happier to see me! I got even closer.

"What happened to you?"

"We can't get home anymore because the current always brings us back here!"

"Don't worry," I told them, "I come from the open ocean, and I know the way! Follow me!"

So slowly, fin stroke after fin stroke,
I helped them swim in the right direction.
At first they struggled, then they picked up the pace and managed to set themselves in the right direction again, overcoming the current and finding their way home.

"THANK YOU, MOKO, WE ARE FOREVER GRATEFUL!"

they said to me before heading out to sea.
I answered them with a jump out of the water. I was so happy for them!

Cher Ami, the Carrier Pigeon

The story of a pigeon who, thanks to his courage, saved many people.

I have always been a great friend of humans. I have a secret agreement with them: They give me lots of good food to eat and, in exchange, I deliver their messages.

I AM A PIGEON AND I REALLY LOVE TRAVELING!

Thanks to my wings I can travel great distances in a short time, and for this reason people have decided to teach me to carry their words around the world.

It works like this: They write a note full of important things, trying to squeeze everything in a few small lines (so much so that even I, sometimes, struggle to read, due to how small they write!).

Then they roll up the piece of paper and tie it delicately to one of my legs.

FINALLY, WHEN EVERYTHING IS READY, I TAKE FLIGHT AND BRING THEIR MESSAGE TO THE DESTINATION, LIKE A MAIL CARRIER DOES!

Unfortunately, a great war broke out. Humans sometimes argue, and they end up doing awful and sad things, which they often later regret.

Why do they do it?

During this great war I was talking about, I was with a group of soldiers who were isolated!

THEY WERE IN THE MIDDLE OF THE BATTLE AND COULD NO LONGER ESCAPE. THEY DIDN'T EVEN HAVE FOOD TO EAT!

I felt tenderness for them, and I felt
I had to help them in some way.
And so I decided to put into practice
what I do best: I took flight with a little help
message tied to my leg!

Once in the air, the enemies tried to stop me,
but they couldn't. I was too fast for them!
They only managed to wound me, but despite
this I resisted and completed my mission.

Thanks to me, many men were saved.

AFTER THAT, I BECOME THEIR
HERO. THEY EVEN GAVE ME
A MEDAL. LOOK HOW
BEAUTIFUL IT IS!

Scarlett, the Brave Cat

The story of a young cat who saved her kittens from a fire.

I would do anything for my kittens. I would even throw myself into flames! And in fact, that's exactly what I had to do. At that time I was a young one-year-old cat and had recently given birth to five beautiful fluffy kittens.

I WAS SO PROUD OF THEM!

I fed them with my milk, stood by them, and kept them safe near me day and night because that's what good cat moms do.

We lived in a garage in the middle of the city, sheltered from possible dangers. There I could watch over my little ones without any problems. It was our home, the family shelter. We were doing well all together, and nothing and no one could harm us.

Unfortunately, however, one morning while I was out looking for something to eat, a big fire broke out in the building where our garage was located.

THE FLAMES WERE SO HIGH, AND WHEN I CAME BACK I SAW THE FIREFIGHTERS BUSY PUTTING OUT THE FIRE!

I dropped the food on the ground and, despite the scorching heat, ran into the flames while the firefighters were trying to tame the fire by spraying water at top speed. It was chaos!

WITH ALL THAT SMOKE, I COULDN'T SEE ANYTHING, BUT I STILL MANAGED TO HEAR THE MEOWS OF MY LITTLE KITTENS AND SNIFFED THEIR SCENT OVER THE ASHES.

I found them huddled in a corner. They were very scared, poor things. There was little time. I had to save them; the flames were coming!

I ran as fast as I could and brought all of my kittens out, one by one. Once I got the last one out, I felt my muzzle and body burning, but I didn't care. I looked around. I had succeeded, I had brought my family to safety!

I SNIFFED THE LITTLE ONES ONE BY ONE, MADE SURE THEY WERE OKAY, THEN COLLAPSED.

When I woke up, I found myself in a different place. Some good humans had taken me and my family to a safe spot. I was so grateful to them! I began to purr as loud as I could, then I looked for my kittens and found them lying beside me.

EVERYBODY WAS BACK WHERE THEY BELONGED.

Lulu, Pig to the Rescue

The story of a little Vietnamese pig who saved her mistress.

It was a day like any other. After eating all my food I was sitting quietly in the living room with Jo-Ann, my mistress.

HOW HAPPY I WAS WITH HER!

She was like my mom, which is why I sat by her side all the time. Our afternoons would fly by! One time—I remember it well—her husband was out and it was just the two of us in the house and our little dog friend in the garden.

All of a sudden, Jo-Ann felt sick. She fell to the floor, struggling to breathe and holding her hands over her heart. She cried out loudly, “Help, help, help!” but no one heard her.

With her last bit of strength she opened the window and shouted again, but still, nothing. What a fright! I didn’t know what to do. I could hear the dog outside, barking as loud as he could, for he, too, realized that Jo-Ann was in danger. Time was passing too quickly!

I HAD TO ACT. I HAD TO HELP HER. THERE WAS NO ALTERNATIVE!

Only another human being could help her, so I gathered my courage and forced my way through the pet door and out of the house.

I BROKE THROUGH THE SMALL GATE THAT SEPARATED ME FROM THE ROAD AND TRIED TO STOP THE CARS THAT WERE SPEEDING BY.

I had hurt myself by knocking down the gate. I had a bad injury but I didn't care. I had to help Jo-Ann at all costs! Cars honked their horns and avoided me, but despite my grunts no one stopped. I was desperate!

I continued undeterred, trying to obstruct the cars, and just when all seemed lost, a good man finally stopped. Yes! This was my chance. I started grunting louder. He looked at my wound and hollered out to see if I had run away. Jo-Ann heard him and shouted back. The man ran toward the house and went inside, and as soon as he saw Jo-Ann on the floor, he called for help. Fortunately, the ambulance arrived quickly, saving her life.

Afterwards I was tired and exhausted, but I had accomplished my mission. All the humans congratulated me, even my dog friend, who barked with happiness

I WILL NEVER FORGET THAT DAY!

Elsa, the Lioness Born Free

The story of a domesticated lioness reintroduced into the wild.

I was very little when it happened. My mother, my sisters Big One and Lustica, and I were in the savannah, under a large bush in the shade. The sun was beating down hard, so that's why we took a rest there. Everything was as slow and sweet as usual, when from afar we heard the sound of a car.

THE HUMANS!

Mom always told us to be careful, so we hid, but they were looking right in our direction.

When they got a few steps away from us, our mother tried to attack them to scare them away. She just wanted to protect us

SUDDENLY WE HEARD A VERY LOUD BANG, AND I CLOSED MY EYES.

I was very scared; there was so much chaos and so much smoke. When I opened my eyes again, mom was on the ground, lifeless. My sisters and I were desperate.

Then one of the men approached us. We tried to run away, but he was faster and caught us. We thought our end had come, but instead, the man, named George, decided to take care of us, together with his wife, Joy. As he took us to his house, he whispered in our frightened ears sweet words. He kept saying “sorry, sorry, sorry” to us.

And so we were adopted by George and Joy. In their home we lacked for nothing: food, water, games, fun, care. They were great parents to us three sisters, who were growing strong and healthy. Only we were growing too much, so reluctantly, George and Joy had to part with two of us, and they decided to bring my sisters, Big One and Lustica, to another place. I, on the other hand, stayed with them. In the meantime, George and Joy had made another decision:

THEY WERE GOING TO TAKE ME BACK TO KENYA AND LET ME LIVE FREE AGAIN, BECAUSE I WAS BORN THAT WAY.

From that moment my training began. My foster parents taught me to hunt, to move in the bush, to stay alive in the wild, how to survive. It was hard training for me, but I felt an instinct inside that urged me not to give up. Finally, when I felt ready, George and Joy took me home.

"GO, ELSA. NOW YOU ARE FREE!"

It was not easy at first, I must admit, but day by day I managed to find my way in the world. I made some mistakes, but I always got back up and found strength in the most precious thing that George and Joy had given me:

FREEDOM.

Oh, I almost forgot; a few years later, my adoptive parents came to visit me . . . and I introduced them to my own three children!

Inky, the Fugitive Octopus

The story of an octopus and his daring escape to freedom.

We octopuses are very intelligent animals. We can solve problems, open jars, find new ways out all the time. We are wizards of escape and disguise! We know how to shrink our size and change color when needed, blending in with the seabed or the rocks so no one can see us when we transform.

SOMETIMES, HOWEVER, IT HAPPENS THAT WE, TOO, MAKE MISTAKES.

And it happened to me. A few years ago, as I was moving placidly at the bottom of the sea, not sensing any danger around me, I suddenly was caught in a net. I tried to wriggle out and escape through the holes, but they were too small! All I could do was hope that no one would hurt me.

I supppose I was lucky. The humans did not kill me, but instead put me in an aquarium. Humans are very curious, and that is one thing they have in common with octopuses:

WE ALSO LIKE TO DISCOVER NEW THINGS.

But I didn't like that aquarium at all. The space was too small. I am an explorer, and being confined in that small cube of water made me sick! I had to come up with something. I had to use my skills to escape!

As the days went by, I studied my surroundings carefully. From my aquarium I observed the room outside until I spotted a small drainpipe through which I could pass. I knew that humans had pipes where they sent waste water to the ocean, and that was where I had to go! First, however, I would have to get out of the cage I was in.

SOONER OR LATER SOMEONE WAS GOING TO MAKE A MISTAKE; IT JUST TOOK PATIENCE ON MY PART . . .

And indeed, one evening, a person did not close the aquarium lid above me properly. Bingo! That was my chance. I waited until everyone was gone, climbed up the glass, and reached the lid. I pushed and shoved it and then jumped out:

AT LAST I WAS FREE!

However, I still had to make the last stretch. Using my tentacles, I moved to the drainpipe, then shrunk down as much as I could to fit through the small pipe. It seemed impossible at first, but I succeeded. How nice to be an octopus! Slowly I slipped into the pipe, and the farther I progressed, the more I tasted the sea water approaching. Finally, after much effort, I made it back to the sea!

AND SINCE THAT DAY I APPRECIATE FREEDOM EVEN MORE.

Sam, the Koala Who Escaped the Fire

The story of a koala rescued from a major fire in Australia.

The forest is my home. I was born and raised there, among the trees, moving from branch to branch, sleeping in the shade of the trees, eating tasty eucalyptus leaves, making friends with other animals.

THAT'S WHY ON THE DAY THE BIG FIRE BROKE OUT, I FELT THE WORLD COLLAPSE ON ME.

One moment, without warning, as I sat as always on a branch eating, I felt a hot gust hit my back. I had felt the heat carried by the wind before, but this time it was different. That air felt like it was burning. Shortly after, down below I saw so many animals fleeing in one direction. I didn't understand what they were fleeing from, but there were all kinds of animals.

EVIDENTLY SOMETHING SERIOUS AND TERRIBLE WAS HAPPENING.

So I became alarmed as well. I tried to peer through the trees, but thick smoke hid my view and prevented me from being able to see far. The smoke then began to take on increasingly red hues. At that point I had no more doubts—it was a fire. I didn't want to believe it! Our forest, our home, was on fire!

I started to run along with the other animals, but the fire was moving so fast, devouring the plants and burning the earth. I felt very hot and was short of breath. I ran as fast as I could, but then

I FELT MY STRENGTH LEAVING ME AND EVERYTHING WENT DARK.

When I woke up I felt pain all over. I was very thirsty, my mouth was dry, and my body was burned. I was still alive, but I was breathing hard. Then, in front of me, as if in a dream, I saw two humans coming toward me.

My vision was poor, as there was still a lot of smoke, but I had no doubt: They were two men in uniform. I usually run away from people, but I had no energy left, so I just sat there, still. To my surprise, one of the men held a small bottle of water and allowed me to quench my thirst. He patted me gently and told me that everything would be all right from then on; they would take care of me

EVEN THOUGH EVERYTHING AROUND ME
WAS ON FIRE, I FELT SAFE AGAIN.

Ning Nong, the Lifesaving Elephant

The story of an elephant who saved a little girl from a tsunami.

Amber and I spend a lot of time together. Although I am a big elephant and she is a little girl, we get along very well! We have many things in common. For example, we both like playing on the beach, running in the sand, and diving in the water. One day–I remember it well–we were in the water as usual, having fun and joking with each other. All of a sudden, however, I saw the water start to recede:

A TSUNAMI WAS COMING–THE BIG WAVE THAT CRASHES INTO THE SHORELINE. WE HAD TO LEAVE RIGHT AWAY!

I tried to get Amber to leave, but she could not understand my nudges and just wanted to stay there and play. I was very worried because we didn't have much time.

THEN, ON THE HORIZON, I SAW THE WAVE COMING.

At that point even Amber understood. We were so scared!

Nevertheless, I gathered my courage. I had to save my little friend, and being so big could come in handy in that situation. In fact, when the water hit us, I managed to keep my feet firmly on the ground while Amber clung to me.

WE COULDN'T HOLD ON FOR LONG, THOUGH . . .

All of a sudden, I heard someone shouting from up on a hill: "Ning Nong! Ning Nong! Quick, come this way!"

He was my master, and he had found us! Following his directions and using all the strength I had in my body, I detached myself from the ground and let the waves carry us toward the hill, swimming to avoid being swept away. I safely kept Amber on top of me at all times, as if I were her life preserver. After much effort, we finally managed to reach high ground and get to safety.

WHAT AN ADVENTURE! AMBER'S MOM WAS OVERJOYED AND THANKED ME SO MANY TIMES. BUT I HAD ONLY DONE MY DUTY AS A FRIEND.

Keiko, the Killer Whale Who Loved Freedom

The story of the killer whale who, after years in captivity, found freedom again.

I was born in the middle of the ocean, surrounded by many other animals, salt water, and most of all, my family. For three years I lived around the islands, grew up, got older, and met many friends.

THEN ONE DAY, HUMANS CAUGHT ME.

I was so sad and scared. I didn't want to leave my home for anything! Yet, the humans never hurt me. They took me to a marine animal park, full of many pools, and taught me things: how to jump, how to hit a ball, how to do twirls in the air, and how to move in a coordinated way underwater, like I was a dancer.

Years went by, and I had become accustomed to my new life. I received food in exchange for the tricks I performed, which everyone seemed to enjoy.

HOWEVER, I MISSED THE OPEN OCEAN AND I MISSED MY HOME.

Most of the time they kept me locked in a small tank; it was very tight and like a prison for me. I felt lonely and sad. Occasionally some dolphins would come to visit me and I was happy, but it was not the same:

I NEEDED MY OCEAN!

After a while, I became a star. Everyone wanted to see me, and they even cast me as the lead in a movie! The story, by the way, was about an orca in a marine animal park returning to freedom.

I DREAMED OF ACTUALLY MAKING THAT JOURNEY AND FINALLY BEING ABLE TO DIVE BACK INTO THE OCEAN, TO BE FREE AGAIN.

The film was a big hit all over the world, and after its release many people were surprised because I, the main character, was living in a marine animal park!

So, some good humans decided to spend money and time to get me away from the prison where I was, to teach me how to go back to nature again, to find food on my own, to be in the middle of the ocean.

SO MANY YEARS HAD PASSED THAT I HAD FORGOTTEN MANY OF THE THINGS I HAD LEARNED WHEN I WAS YOUNG.

Despite everything, step by step—or, fin by fin—I managed to regain my instincts. I was so excited! No more tanks, no more prisons. The good humans took me back to the ocean where I was born, and I was finally free again.

Sniffer and Tinni, Different but the Same

The story of a fox and a dog who became best friends.

SNIFFER: My name is Sniffer, and I'm a fox!

TINNI: My name is Tinni, and I am a dog!

SNIFFER: We met for the first time in my home, the forest. Tinni was with her master. I usually run away from both humans and dogs, but those two were different from the others.

TINNI: I remember the first time I saw Sniffer. He was wandering around with his head down sniffing the damp forest floor, looking for something to munch on. That reddish ball of fur hadn't even noticed us until he raised his head.

SNIFFER: What a scare! They were so close, and I was so focused on finding food that I didn't notice them . . . I stopped immediately, fearing the worst.

TINNI: Yes, Sniffer was really scared, but neither I nor my master had any intention of hurting her. On the contrary! She was beautiful and we just wanted to get to know her better.

SNIFFER: I remember Tinni came to me slowly, wagging her tail and conveying calmness. All I could do was let her come closer, I couldn't have run away anyway. When she came within a couple of feet of me, I came forward, too, shy and awkward.

TINNI: We sniffed and immediately liked each other! We found that we liked the same things: running in the forest, rolling in the mud, jumping over ditches, resting in the shade of the big plants. So we became friends!

SNIFFER: Tinni and her master visit me very often, and I am always happy. Tinni and I have become inseparable. As soon as we see each other we hug and immediately start playing. How nice to have a special friend like her!

TINNI: I have never met any animal as special as Sniffer. We are so different, yet at heart we are the same! The friendship between a dog and a fox is something incredible!

Sniffer: I agree!

Hachiko, the Dog Who Waits

The story of a dog who for years has been waiting for his master to return.

I stay here and wait. My master always comes back. I know his schedule; every morning I walk him to the station at the same time.

EVERY AFTERNOON I GO BACK AND WAIT FOR HIM AT THE RIGHT TIME.

He gets off the usual train and hugs me, and together we go back to our home. That is why I am still here waiting for him:

I KNOW HE WILL COME BACK SOONER OR LATER.

I met my master when I was just a puppy. He chose me out of so many other dogs, and I will be grateful to him forever.

HE GAVE ME LOVE AND PROTECTION FROM DAY ONE, AND I RECIPROCATED WITH LOTS OF CUDDLES AND FUN TIMES.

We have always been inseparable, my master and I. And for that very reason I will never stop waiting for him at the station. Even though he hasn't been around for years.

On an afternoon like any other, I went to the station, but to my surprise he did not get off the usual train. I thought that, due to some mishap, he had caught the next train, so I waited. Nothing. I came back the next day and the day after that. I have been doing that for years now.

I'M NOT GOING TO GIVE UP. SOONER OR LATER HE WILL COME BACK. HE ALWAYS DOES.

So many people, meanwhile, have become attached to and care for me. I am grateful to each one of them. I feel they love me; they bring me food when I'm hungry, water when I'm thirsty, and blankets when it's cold. They pet me and keep me company while I wait for my master to return.

BECAUSE SOONER OR LATER HE WILL RETURN, I AM SURE.

Meanwhile, some humans have
even built a statue in my honor.

IT IS VERY BEAUTIFUL AND LOOKS A LOT LIKE ME.

That bronze dog looks like my twin brother. They told me that the statue is for me, for what I am doing, for my loyalty.

I, HOWEVER, DIDN'T QUITE UNDERSTAND WHAT I DID THAT WAS SO SPECIAL TO DESERVE IT. AFTER ALL, I'M JUST A DOG WAITING.

Magawa, the Bomb-Sniffing Rat

The story of a rat who helped save countless lives.

No one is as good as me when it comes to finding landmines. Yes, this is my job. Every morning I get up and help humans get all the bad things that have been buried under the ground out of the way.

BUT WHY DO HUMANS HAVE TO ACT THIS WAY? CAN'T THEY ALL JUST GET ALONG?

Now, though, someone has to take those bombs out. And I am so good at finding them!

Yes, they chose me, a giant rat; with my unerring sense of smell I can sniff out bombs underground.

THEY HAVE TRAINED ME TO RECOGNIZE THEIR SMELL, AND I AM NOW AN EXPERT!

Every day I am taken to large fields littered with mines–they are everywhere! I move cautiously, knowing that I have a nice advantage: My long, slender body is lighter than the heavy, clumsy bodies of humans, so I can walk through the bombs and even step on them, without detonating them. One after another, in the course of my career I have found more than a hundred bombs.

I AM MUCH BETTER THAN A DETECTOR!

Men buried them during the war to defeat enemies; now that the war is over, it's my turn to find them to prevent anyone from getting hurt.

I ENJOY MY WORK SO MUCH.

I know that I can be useful and save many lives, and for me this is a source of immense joy. Although I do hope that my job, in the future, will no longer exist. Because it will mean that mines will no longer exist either!

I smell the earth and walk among the fields, while men look at me and give me medals–they are so proud of me and everything I do for them. This is what I would like to tell them:

I DON'T NEED MEDALS! ALL I WOULD LIKE IS FOR YOU TO STOP FIGHTING, ONCE AND FOR ALL. THAT WOULD BE THE GREATEST GIFT IN THE WORLD.

Laika, the Little Astronaut Dog

The story of the little dog who traveled into space.

Yes sir, they really chose me for this mission! My name is Laika, and I love to travel. I was born in a big city, but I never had a real family.

UNTIL I WAS THREE YEARS OLD, I WAS ON MY OWN, WANDERING THE STREETS. I LEARNED TO GET BY ON THE STRENGTH OF MY PAWS!

I met many other stray dogs like me, and together we formed a good team to defend ourselves from danger, to resist the cold, and to find something to eat. Of course, though, I would have preferred a nice warm and cozy home . . .

One day, some men caught me; I was always afraid of humans and tried to run away, but although I was running very fast, they caught up with me and took me off the road!

I WAS VERY SCARED. I DIDN'T KNOW WHAT THEY WERE GOING TO DO TO ME. I FEARED THE WORST.

Instead, the humans turned out to be good to me. They fed me, cared for me, gave me a home and a roof over my head. Finally, I was no longer suffering from the cold! The road, however . . . I kind of missed it.

AS I MENTIONED, I LIKE TO TRAVEL A LOT!

When I lived outside I could go wherever
I wanted; now I was safe, but with fewer places
to explore, so I didn't think twice when some men
approached me and said,

"LAIKA, WOULD YOU LIKE TO GO ON A LONG TRIP?"

I barked and wagged my tail.
I was overjoyed! The trip was the most incredible of all; it involved going directly into space, among the stars! No living being had ever been up there, so I was proud to be the first ever. I was trained for space flight, and everything was explained to me in great detail.

I FOLLOWED THE PROGRAM TO PERFECTION.

On the day of the launch I was very nervous, but once the rocket took off, I looked down and was amazed–everyone had all gotten so small! Then I looked up and in front of me I saw only one thing:

INFINITE SPACE. MILLIONS OF STARS, BRIGHT DOTS ON A BIG BLUE EXPANSE, AND THEN THE MOON, THE SUN, AND THE PLANETS.

Traveling in my little rocket, I had become part of the sky, as if I were a bright star myself.

Jonathan, the Long-Lived Tortoise

The story of the world's oldest tortoise.

My name is Jonathan, and I am a tortoise. We tortoises take life very slowly. We don't like to run.

WE PREFER TO GO SLOW . . . SLOW . . . SLOW . . .

We like to walk in the middle of green meadows and eat slowly, savoring every little morsel, but most of all, we tortoises love to sleep a lot. In our life there is no hurry.

I was probaby born around the year 1800, and today I live on a small island in the middle of the ocean. Everywhere I turn I see water, a big blue expanse. Looking at the distant horizon helps me to be calm. I don't really remember the day of my birth; it's been so long . . .

SOME PEOPLE SAY THAT I AM MORE THAN TWO HUNDRED YEARS OLD! UNBELIEVABLE, ISN'T IT?

And you would think a two-hundred-year-old tortoise would be old, but no way! I'm in great shape.

Of course, I don't see as well now as I did when I was just hatched out of the egg. But I can still tell the difference between a lettuce leaf and a sheet of newspaper. I can hardly smell but it doesn't matter.

I HAVE SEVERAL KIND PEOPLE TAKING CARE OF ME.

Together with me, on the same . . . the same . . . the same . . . where was I? Ah, yes! On the same island, three of my friends live together with me: Emma, David, and Fred.

I LIKE TO SPEND TIME WITH THEM BECAUSE WE SHARE THE SAME PASSIONS. AND SO WE SPEND OUR DAYS IN. . .

Man, I must have fallen asleep . . . sorry! What was I going to say? Um . . . oh, yes! When I was growing up, the world was completely different.

THERE WERE NO TELEPHONES, NO TELEVISION, NO CARS. THERE WEREN'T EVEN PHOTOGRAPHS.

Now, on the other hand, so many people take pictures of me and wish me a long, long, long life. It is enough for me to continue doing what I enjoy every day.

George and Mabel, Two Crows in Love

The love story of two crows who fight together against adversity.

When crows choose a mate, we keep them for life, just like in a marriage.

EVEN IF WE DON'T OFFICIALLY GET MARRIED, WE ALWAYS STAY FAITHFUL!

Just like my partner, George, and I (Mabel), despite adversity. The important thing for us is to stay together. No matter what happens.

And things, I assure you, happened to us a lot! Together we have overcome the heat of summer and even the frost of winter. George and I have always shared everything–first and foremost food:

EATING TOGETHER IS OUR ABSOLUTE FAVORITE THING.

We live in a beautiful garden full of trees where we can rest, but most importantly where we have built our nest. Slowly, a little at a time, we took turns bringing twigs and intertwining them until we built the house of our dreams. At that point we decided to start a family.

AND AN EGG SPROUTED IN THE CENTER OF THE NEST.

Then one day, while I was in the nest incubating our little egg, George came home with a broken beak:

IT WAS REALLY BROKEN; I WAS SCARED FOR HIM!

I asked him what happened, and he told me he had hit a branch because of a strong gust of wind. Eating, for George, had become more difficult. He had to bend down to pick up crumbs and seeds, but despite this he did not give up and continued to bring food to me as well. I always trusted him, never doubting his qualities, AND he never betrayed me. Yes,

MY PARTNER IS A TRUE HERO.

When our little one was born, our problems suddenly disappeared. From that moment we only had eyes for our baby. Winters no longer frighten us; not even accidents along the way have stopped us.

OUR FAMILY IS CLOSER THAN EVER. AND GEORGE AND I ARE MORE AND MORE IN LOVE!

Koko, the Gorilla Who "Speaks"

The story of a gorilla who learned sign language.

I am a gorilla, but I can also talk to humans. Yes, you heard me right:

I CAN TALK TO THEM AND COMMUNICATE WITH SIGNS.

My friend Francine, who has been taking care of me since I was a baby, taught me this. I live in a reserve with other gorillas, and Francine spends a lot of time with me. Even when she was very young herself, she treated me like I was her own, trying to explain things to me, showing me the right way to express what I was feeling.

And so, for me, it has always been very easy to understand human beings. Francine and I talk about everything; she has taught me so many things.

THANKS TO HER HELP I CAN COMMUNICATE WITH HUMANS, TELLING THEM HOW I FEEL: SAD, HAPPY, TIRED, EXCITED.

I do this through sign language. Each sign is associated with a certain word. Very simple! And today, thanks to her, I can say what I want and make myself understood. No other animal is like me, and I know I am special because of that.

I also know that I am a gorilla, but I like to be with humans. I have even picked up some of their habits; for example, I adopted a cat!

I REALLY ENJOY SPENDING TIME WITH THIS PURRING BALL OF FUR THAT SLEEPS NEXT TO ME, SOFT AND GENTLE.

I even gave him a name: All Ball, because I love to rhyme! I pet him and treat him like part of my family; I really love him very much.

Thanks to the words Francine taught me, I am also able to joke and make humans laugh. How nice when I am the one who triggers their laughter!

THANKS TO THESE QUALITIES OF MINE, I BECAME FAMOUS ALL OVER THE WORLD, AND SEVERAL CELEBRITIES CAME TO VISIT ME.

And of course I was able to talk to them as well! Did I mention that I love to talk? Hmm, I think so!

Like all stories, even the best ones have an ending. The important thing is that it be a happy one!

And now we come to the conclusion of our journey. We rode a sled together with Balto, jumped into the water with Dindim and his friends, and then applauded the dolphin Moko for his great selfless gesture. Cher ami made us fly high; Scarlett the cat taught us that with courage and love, any obstacle can be overcome. So did little pig Lulu, another heroine of our stories!

And then there were the tales of freedom, like the one about the lioness Elsa, the octopus Inky, and the killer whale Keiko! And of course we can't forget about Sam the koala and her rescue by brave and strong humans, as well as Ning Nong, the elephant protagonist of a heroic act during a tsunami!

New friendships were born along the way; some should be remembered, such as the special and unexpected one between the fox Sniffer and the dog Tinni, or the wonderful and poignant one between Hachiko and his master.
Magawa the rat has been a friend to humans and helped them save so many lives. And then there is Laika, the little dog who dreamed big and reached outer space, while the tortoise Jonathan watched from the ground as he chewed slowly . . . slowly . . . slowly . . .
There's also the beautiful love story between the crows George and Mabel, an extraordinary and very strong couple! Finally we met Koko, the intelligent gorilla who accompanied us to the end of the trip.

Now all that remains is to say goodbye, but this is not really goodbye! The world is full of stories about extraordinary animals! We must keep our eyes open to find them and our hearts ready to welcome them.

SEE YOU SOON WITH MANY MORE STORIES!

ILLUSTRATOR

Bianca Austria produces playful and whimsical art around themes like wildlife, exploration, and travel. She takes pride in using art to empower her Filipino culture as well as other underrepresented communities. Her work has been featured by Disney and *The New Yorker*. She has also received awards from the Society of Illustrators in New York and The One Club for Creativity.

AUTHOR

Leonardo Mazzeo began his career in the world of communication by collaborating with various online publications on short stories and novels. Always passionate about nature, he is the creator and editor of the *Bestiale* newsletter, which collects curiosities and incredible stories from the animal world.

WS whitestar kids™ is a trademark of White Star s.r.l.

Piazzale Luigi Cadorna, 6 - 20123 Milan, Italy
www.whitestar.it

Editing: Michele Suchomel-Casey

First printing, August 2025

ISBN 978-88-544-2160-8
1 2 3 4 5 6   29 28 27 26 25

Printed and manufactured XY Cultural and Creative Park,
Huangpu District, Guangzhou, China

FSC www.fsc.org
MIX
Paper | Supporting responsible forestry
FSC® C178000